The Owl
Behind
The Door

Stanley Cooperman

McClelland and Stewart Limited
TORONTO / MONTREAL

The Owl
Behind
The Door

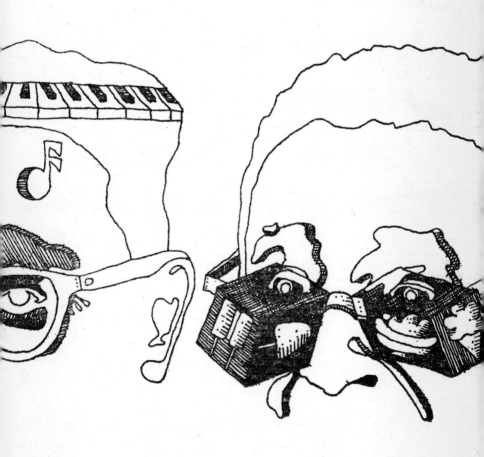

The Canadian Publishers
McClelland and Stewart Limited
25 Hollinger Road, Toronto 16

DESIGN: *Don Fernley*
DRAWINGS: *Gord Oglan*

PRINTED AND BOUND IN ENGLAND BY
HAZELL WATSON AND VINEY LTD
AYLESBURY, BUCKS

for Esta, Lil, Jenifer, Habibi,
and
Cappelbaum

Books by Stanley Cooperman:

WORLD WAR I AND THE AMERICAN NOVEL,
The John Hopkins Press, 1967

THE DAY OF THE PARROT and Other Poems,
University of Nebraska Press, 1968

Contents

Part 2

Part 3

Part 1

when the merry-go-round horse
went   up   and never
came down

12

Everything I do is a kind
of eating:
      I swallow
you, and spit out green
flowers, the shape
of your nose
becomes a syllable
planted deeper
than the roots of trees,
and when I cry, my
tears
are chocolate sodas   sucked
through the straw shape
of a poem.

Never trust a man with
a typewriter
between his lips:
when we kiss, I watch the meaning
of your secret breath
in a mirror;
I make love
on glass, and sprawl
in a hundred ways
to learn the truth
about the back of your head
while my tongue
plunges
      full
into your mouth.

Watch me squint when I suffer
or laugh: my feet
find razor-blades
in happy grass,
and broken bones are
jokes,
toothpicks
goosing a giraffe. . . .

Don't go through my wallet:
I've been sleeping
with all your best friends,
their fathers,
and the neighbor's
pregnant dog;
when I leave the house
I point
in every direction,
                    rolling
like a crazy compass,

a sun-dial
always at high noon.

14

In a world of bright wind,
Mary-Anne,
why are your eyes so pale?
Somewhere inside you
a door
is always locked,
and a hand
flaps on the empty wood.

What can I do for you,
Mary-Anne?
How can I unwrinkle
your dream?

Look at the world:
shapes of leaves and round
mouths
roll to a touch. . .
red balloons, and mountains,
and God
      rubbing himself
on the other side of the moon.

That man who rode you down:
his hooves
were harmless as snow
blown on the sea;
his arms held nothing,
not even
> the woman
> that you are now.

I wish I could do something for you,
Mary-Anne,
if not as friend,
then as lover:
I wish I could plant tigers
under your hair, until

the sound of their feeding
would be all
> you could hear.

A Riddle

16   The meaning of the first letter
        is red, heavy
        as peonies after rain,
        or the sound of breath
        in a dark room.

        The second is blue, like
        the pause
        just before we touch
        a woman's skin, wondering
        if our fingers
        will laugh at us, or if she
        will turn
        round
        inside our hands.

        The third letter is
        green, a cloud distended
        over wet landscapes,
        where oceans
        slide
        into the mouths of trees.

        The fourth is a white bird
        hatching
                stones, a parrot
        paler than soap, crying
        for jungles
        behind the bathroom sink.

And there was. . .
night
waiting behind the rose-bush,
laughing worms
and the heavy dream
of a snail.

This is how I understand
creation:
when I eat something good
or water the lawn,
when I touch your new scar
or move my finger
through the quiet
hair
growing on your thighs,

I understand
that I
      exist, am
to be counted among the facts
of the world, like
stars
and wooden fences;
and all the mysterious business
under my skin

is no monologue, is
somehow
         a duet, with God
and green birds
shaking their
feathers
on a silver roof.

18

I seem to spend all my time
looking for jewels
in my nostrils,
climbing under my own tongue
and arguing
with yesterday's dinner.

It's a soliloquy
without a play,
a dialogue
in an empty room
where all the windows
have turned
blank.

I try to listen to
you, but
my ears are filled
with something else, an echo
from a mouth
inside my brain, and
everywhere
I go it follows me
complaining
that I forgot something,
      somewhere,

a bill that I didn't pay,
or the gold ring
that fell through my
poem
when the merry-go-round horse
went   up   and never
came down.

It's like talking
under water, and when you
stare at me,   hurt
because I never see anything
past the edge
of my eyeballs,
all I can do is offer
this:

     a kind of wine-bottle
     filled
     with red flowers.

I am a stranger here, my passport
is no damn good,
there is something
terribly wrong
in my veins,
dogs
and old men
have stolen my bed:

why do you blame me for arguing?
why do you hate
the shape
of my only dream?   or the night
growing
under my clothes?

Why do you assume that I eat fireflies
when mushrooms
cover my teeth?

Look at my face: there are holes
in my skin, eyes
nose
          a mouth
and something that leaks
into the dark
every time I look at you, or
breathe.

True, I never
march
anywhere, never stand up
to be COUNTED for anything

except   maybe   the sign
of dust
under my tongue,

because when I see the edge of my hands
it is fearful
country,
that border
of nails reaching
into space, pink

weeds, and the question
of what
          ends where. . .
or begins: like moths
between your lips
when you try

to tell me who dances
inside
          your head, and why.

A Cablegram for Leonard Cohen

Cohen,
what are you doing in Hydra?

Hydra   the snake.

Is this what happens when grandfathers
turn grant, and gas-
chambers

vanish in puffs of
ink, a fine powder
covering all the skullcaps
of the world?

What do you dream of
in Hydra?

Do you hunt wolves among the stones,
or sleep with mermaids
wearing *shetels*
on their sea-weed hair?

I worry about you, Cohen:
there is a smell of fish
and fried crabs
in the air, and when
I read your poems

a hook-nosed angel
plays the bouzookie in corners
of my house,
plucking each string
with his beard.

What do you wear on your forehead
when the sun
                sprays olives
down on the beach?

Do you write your poems
with a ram's horn
dipped
in the jeweled blood
of goats?

Here is a gift
from me, I
send it to you from another island
filled with temples
and Ladies
                Auxiliaries,
a gift from a muddy
ocean
to the white foam
of your exile:

It is a golden shoelace
to tie
our feet together
when we run

(spitting paper)

past fringes of the horizon, looking
for honey

                in the heavy wool
                of our tears.

Nocturne for a Mexicali Motel

24   Never
is an always thing
at midnight   when you can't
sleep,
and the moon
breaks into pieces of
private stone
under your eyes,

or the air (strained
by two other
lungs) waits for
something: animals
looking for a place to hide,
apes
picking bananas
behind the closet,

waiting for vines to open in the sleeves
of your coat: listen
to the way they   mumble
with hair
in their mouths, and

when they shuffle their
gums, listen
to the sound of leaves,
time
making green circles
between the walls
of your
          sheets. . . .

Pastoral

Your fingers may stroll with mine   25
on that fair surface, the meadow
whose name we share;
silk may grow like cultivated lawn
sweet as the moon we wrap in glass
(when lovers dance on each other's crust
pouring roses from their eyes
as though each blossom were a meteor-stone
immortal as arithmetic). . . .

But certain hollowness, or fluid
thickening in time,
draws the roots of secret hair
down to a level of lava-blood
erupting beneath the skin:
a boiling we can hear
rapid and delicate, yet
heavy-footed as the stars. . . .

the sound of small birds drowning
or mice eaten by green owls.

Serenade for a Cubed Eyeball

"Deer do not climb trees" – JAMIE REID

Deer climb trees,
always
climb trees: they move
through forests of green
snow, their hooves
sharper
than angels; they breathe
the meaning of spider-
web and moss, their noses
roll
through space like puffs of wet
black   love

Deer climb trees,
always
climb trees: their nerve-
endings find secret ways between
raindrops, the delicate
hairs
growing inside their brain
rattle and bang like
a million television wires
singing
on all the rooftops of the world.

Deer climb trees,
always
climb trees,
blinking from mushrooms to leaves,
lashing surprised squirrels
who stare
from sudden holes
with walnuts and sugar-cubes
stuck
in their throats.

(and a poet in skinny pants,
a psychedelic shirt
pinned
to his skinless back,
leather dreams
rubbing his shinbones,
jerks through dead books,
weeds, and a tangle
of pubic hair:
even fire-flies   vomit
at the glitter of canned
glass
in his mouth)

Deer climb trees,
always
climb trees,
but not for any poet
falling out of his own skull
like a frozen ape,
stomping
rotted angels
with somebody else's boots. . . .

he drifts
through the wet whisper
of the living grass
on borrowed knuckles.

28

In sleep, a taste
of saliva
like new wine
from burning grapes,
fire
out of bone,
children
or worms
marching to familiar drums;

In sleep, a dance
of metal
sprayed on nursery-grounds,
a pasture
of rock, where goats
scream
the name of God
from a hundred mouths
filled with holiness and blood;

In sleep, a figure
wrapped in old newspapers, knives
piercing his tongue,
stumps of lovers
planted with rice,
their history
becoming
dirt
under rotten nails. . .

It's a nightmare
      not
           of my choosing,

and when I wake up scared,
looking
for you, there is
nothing,
only my eyelids pinned
to my skull,
and a dog
barking
in the empty street of your smile.

Let Solomon argue
with all of his wives,
and scream about goats
in his father's bed;

I know something
that Solomon never
(when he slept on a bed
of golden wire
and dreamed of knives
or harps in his fever)

thought to plant
on the thousand thighs
that circled his palace
and danced in his head:
I know why

the hairs on his neck
cracked and opened
under his coat,
why his brocade collar
pressed with jewels,
and the buttons carved

in the shape of birds
(a peacock drowned
in the folds of his skin)
clapped their claws
and prayed to the moon,

shook their beaks
in a Hebrew holler,
and rained dry figs
down on the mouths
of the brown lions
at the city gate;

I know why, when the boys
came home, Solomon sat
on his high-back throne

shaking olive-pits in a bowl
of oiled fur and animal-bone,
cursing the laps
of his thousand wives,

      and pulling the marrow
      out of a rose.

The Juggler

32

I danced down the street
carrying God in one hand
and a green rattle
in the other.

The rattle was filled
with the frozen spit
of angels:
it made the sound of sand.

Covering the corners of buildings
were my neighbors,
their faces
polished into grains
blown by the wind.

I danced, and shook
my instrument
at the empty spaces of their eyes,
until a pulse leaped
in their arms, their joints.

They followed me, tossing
pennies, and God
snapped up each coin,
putting it
neatly

into a purse of mud.

Carnival at Mt. Whistler

An old Indian dancing before or after beer-bottles,
his moccasins hanging from the sky.

The chairlift is working, and God
spreads over the slopes
with a grin of wet snow.

Sometimes, when the wind is wrong,
a smell of engine oil
drifts over the stumps of fir trees and smiles,
and yesterday's lovers rub grease over their parts.

From this slope
marked with a blue dot (for experts only)
you can see the mountains
of spectacular country, where
everyone tries to be blond.

Tonight, a barbeque: tonight ski-pants
will stretch, young men
will flex their conditions, olders
will hold their balance with both hands,
caught by a sudden edge
on a slope that goes down, and down,

like a waterfall
filled with frozen money.

34

Fig-
ments of trees projected
on skin, like canvas
stretched
between our arms, a sound-
track   paved
with snakes or dry
jelly-beans, lovers picking
their teeth with
crucifixes,
and on the right side
of yesterday's rib,
a lullaby for
                everybody.

Why should we remember
                it?

I mean   why   should we look
for snapdragons
inside our socks?
When I open my mouth, the
sun
comes down
with a million bugs
I can't even see,
with legs
and invisible hairs
running around my lungs,
and even your   name
is a puff
of vibrating space.

It's not that I hate
the taste, but
why make a *megilleh* out of
sunflower seeds,
or reasons
for the sound of a grape
squished between
my fingers?

Why should I manufacture
candles
when I tumble through the world
dancing   on the wax

from my own beard?

Jenifer's Song

36   Do we live
in "a chaos of the sun?"
is that it?
              Chaos?
why, with this hand
I make it pattern, your breast
perhaps, setting up
a sequence
of whispering nerves,
rhymes
under your skin:
and the random charge
gathers, flows through the right
channels, swelling
finally
to this pink point
rolled between my thumbs. . . .

No, this
is not chaos: you
follow my hand
like a river
follows a cleft of granite,
the stone
softer than water. . . .
and the shape of sudden
roundness
on your mouth
is an arrangement, one
molecule
among a million dancing stars
alive
in their own burning.

Stillwell Avenue

On green velvet
where pale men whisper
under cat-light,
he offers a check-list
of women,
pneumatic honeycombs
whitening the moon.

Rolling ivory
among shadows, he
suggests
(keeping his voice
in his pocket)
Betty-Jo, ushered
burning from the Bijou
for love
in the projection room.

On green velvet
he sets his cue
remembering Lucille
who drifted
into wine-bottles:
she now uncorks
at the sign
of the Dutch cigar.

With chalk
on their eyelids
pale men
figure
a memory of odds,
their hands clean
above the quiet
    triangles.

38

Wisdom is
the result of
hawks
squatting on eggs
made of stone
and green
fire.

Wisdom is
perfection broken
into the
     shape
of clouds, and a million
tongues
swollen at high
   noon.

Your wisdom
is composed of those small
nerves
under your eyelids,
the gentle
hair
near your arms.

Sometimes
when you talk
to me
I hear the noses
of all the Rabbis
of the world
coughing snuff at the walls
of Jericho, the
moat
of the moon, and

their wives who
sell
    fish.

Wisdom is the market-
place
of our dreams,
stalls turned over
by Cossacks who carry
white clubs
in their
        mustaches,
the sound of
books
grinding together like
    teeth.

Yahrzeit: On Haifa Beach

40

Shatter the deepest flesh of us
with vibration
of concentric blue:
the ram's horn calls return
to a landscape
simple
as spilled blood.

Cut us adrift,
refract us into sound;
let sacraments and sea-
fingers
stitch our lips
with weeds.

Grind us into rock,
father
of foam,
grind us into
bridegrooms, wed us
to salt:

fill our hands with
stones,
and our dreams
fill
with unwritten scrolls: a *minyon*
of dead rabbis, their
debates melted

into broken candles,
a thin wailing from the North.

Charlotte in Oregon

White birds,
   a sky
filled with swans,
sea-lions
            looking
for caves,
mountains like
nipples
larger than any farm. . . .

You claimed the continent
like a small thing
in a cage
built for giants.
Frozen wind
and echoes
beneath your hand
made hymns
where no voice could grow:
shapes of foam
among salt-
driven leaves.

I remember
how your hair stretched wide
over highways
of unpainted space,
a revelation of
Methodist
whales,

and I remember
that when you turned again,
admitting the necessity
of me,
        I had long since
drifted
into sand.

42

See: these are the motions
of my mouth: shapes
bite
your neck,
     turn
and in mid-space
stomp the battered belly
of a flea. . . .

You
with yellow hair
and the fire
behind: why
should thighs be stained
with ink? What
does that paper mean
rolled between the
pink
     flint of your knees?

Past my window
there are
                still
roses
swallowed by green things,
leaves curl
in the jaws of the moon,
and cats
chase mourning worms
through compost
at the edge of the grass. . . .

I have not read a book
for months, I
have sinned, spitting secret
dreams
at my neighbor's wife:
I have drifted
under the carpet, looking
for signs. . . .

Why do you think
I speak to you with the singing
meat
        of my brain?

44

When the moon is
yellow, wolves
and skinny animals
point
their noses
at the stars, and husbands
wait
behind geraniums
for strange girls, thin
as light.

When the rain
stops
in the Northwest
flowers grow thick
every night: spring comes
late, a cluster
of grapes seeded with
kisses,
a kind of orange
cropped from the snow.

When yucca plants
tickle the sky, their white
smell
filling the spaces
between fir-trees,
a man can look at himself
and count the petals
growing
like hair
from the nape of his dream. . . .

It's a restless season,
long delayed:
Alaska
is far away
on a night like this,
and if you hold your ear
close
to your skin,
you can hear the rush
of a continent,

a year
of forgotten rivers,
and salmon
like fat tongues
in the sea.

46   I wonder what silence
      hears like, said
      the small animal feeding
      beneath my tongue;
      this vault now, my
      natural
      accommodation of forever-
      squeeze
      is of time
      certainly the final
      and most pink
      YES,
      which
      therefore
      indicates a Lord of Push
      who
      swallows
      patterns for my
      sucking self,
      a gentle func-
      tion not to be defined
      by any tic-toc:
      for my
      love
      is wise in mandibles,
      blood-blossoms
      blessed beyond all
      metronomes
      or numbers.

      O sweet
      combustible composted
      there!
      I listened too, and
      heard
      between the root and vessel
      of the weave,
      redness
      winking in the dark.

The Heretic

Have I ever bothered   47
you?

Seriously.

Why
does it mean, if
I
choose
to dance in the cave of
my own nostril?

You sit there
smoking
like an ape with its ass on fire,
nervous, in-
flamed
about something

everything,

eating barbed-wire spaghetti
and crying at the taste
of rust
in the sauce.

Why does my mouth
scare you?

Is it my fault if all the cooks
in the world
use dirty spoons?

All I eat
is my own grass, salted
with snow, and sometimes a red
leaf,

Am I hurting anybody?

48

The three
mouths
of God
are filled
with apples,
lions,
and whales.

In the first,
a taste
of stone
pressed to sweetness,
a swift
crunch
of thighs.

In the second,
yellow
hair
stretched between
the jaws
of trees,
a yawn
of dried blood.

In the third,
fat
dreams
drifting
on the ocean,
swallowing
grease. . . .

The three
mouths
of God
argue with
each other,
and spit
flowers
at the stars.

They open to
show
tongues
like damp
sheets,
and the taste
of something
black.

50

Nothing

is the shape of an egg,
a balloon
of blue feathers:
two hands
and a thumb

over the moon.

Nothing

is where you walk
unburied in your skin,
bits of the sky swallowed
by roosters

(who dig for worms
in their
   wives).

Nothing
is a space set between two
commas,
a circle of white   wood
beaten flat between the
jaws of machines

and poets.

Nothing
is

the laughter of glands, a re-
flection
without mirrors,
a dance
on the edge of your fingers,

> where heavy
> flamencos

> drink
> their own water.

Part 2

What kind of music
do you want to play
on the holes
of your skin?

54

Grief
is a kind of boredom,
an empty place
in a wall covered with books,
or the famous
                author
who cried on the grass
in front of the student union
when the sun
rolled around screaming
through fir-trees.

My own
grief arrives
with a blast of
violins,
a whiteness inside
my head, a lack
of anything definite: no enemies
I care to hate, and thickness
settling down like
a quilt
behind my eyebrows.

I would welcome even
a sneeze, or something to hurt
my teeth, but
my mouth is quiet,
filled
        as usual
with the shape of my tongue;
the light   stops
at the start of my hands,
and my veins stay
where they belong, under
the skin.

Actually, I have nothing
to complain about,
there are
birds
     composed
by my window,
and the pear-tree is blooming
in the garden, I feel
its petals
under my collar, and
the evening
has come at the right time
for
    evening, and dinner
is not burnt: so

why
do I hear
those violins, like
animals
eating something
under my bed?

There it is, a circle
of idiot
          space

bulging
with its own
nothing,

with Professors
wearing

Charles Olson's pajamas;

There it is, round
as a Mexican
sun
          filled
with broken wind,

a feather
popped from the bombulations
of knock-

kneed unicorns;

It is, of course, a shape:
a man
with purple

balloons
between his legs,
blowing   up
flat tires
every time he sits. . .

Circles: they
hang
from heavy lips
like lolly-
pops

or poems

bounced
against sticky mirrors,
a jelly of
          disciples and
          members.

Circles are:
Campus
Missionaries, waiting

under trees with bits

of paper
in their gullets,

coughing ex-
communications at each other.

If you see them oozing
over the horizon
or under

your rug, remember
how they

explode
into pieces of old rubber
at the poke of any

single
finger, or the stomp
of an untied

foot.

58

There is no end
to this   arrangement,
it can go on longer than leaves,
longer than mechanics
dreaming of the moon,
longer than salesmen
cursing
the snow
when it comes down from the mountain
with a smell of unsold
whales.

What kind of music
do you want to play
on the holes
of your skin?

Slowly: check out your LIFE
VALUES
before joining the band;
list your
              reasons
before walking on the grass
singing
with all your toes: remember that

everyone is
listening, everyone plucks
ears
from the falling sky,
and they circle each other
with broken fiddles
under their eye-
bones.

Be careful   be
anything but silk,   because
tubas are pumping
the stars away, and whatever
touches
has nails bigger than
fists, serious
notes
pressed into woolen pockets
waiting for the end
of the world, a crazy itch

arranged
by Conductors who
march across oceans,
landscapes
planted with patriots, teachers
and hungry
                animals. . .

The Retreat

60   Let bough down summers come
with knees and apples,
rockets green
as girls;
breeding in meadows
are all the days
of our deaths,
and we glow in august
celebration
of melting
grass.

So
sweet moonstroke
I dangle
you, and praise
the acid flow
of your lover's
dark;
drinking apricots
and riding white horses
around the nape
of your splendid never-
ness, I think
of snapdragons. . . .

Here
is a cool and thirsty place,
room enough
for all arithmetic
of rings and dying worlds:
one by one
my kisses
make small shapes,
dropped like
pebbles
into standing water.

Canticle in Praise of Green Music

(for J. Michael Yates)

What kind of boast is this?   **61**
to run through the world
backward?

Why should a man
hang from his own anus
with iron fingers?

Anything so heavy
lies: an eye
trying to become stone,

or a bird dropped into space
with all its feathers
glued to the bone.

       The man with the brass intestine
       squeezes barbed wire
       from the closed holes of his face.

       He blows cubes of silence
       from his nostrils, like a whale
       trapped in a dry river.

       He bulges through August
       in search of mud,
       afraid that the dance of any summer

       will crack his skin.

A physician,
  a Turk
with brown eyes:
      almonds
stuck
in his face,
and words
like honey
oozing from the nose
of God.

Robed in his own
lashes
he looks at women,
remembering
  secret places,
globes
of pus and sweet
apricots
under their skirts. . . .

always
   a slow
stroking, some poems
sung
by dead fools,
and between the sheets
of his smile
a hump
of strange camels
     feeding
on something rubbed.

Who speaks of the Promised Land?
horizons
of ripe dung?
mountains
heavy as silk?
the dancer weaving blue
carpets
with his lips?

    I offer you this
         physician,
a Specialist in obstetrics,
gynecology,   and
           LOVE.

64

Each thing:
the man with the white sword,
lovers
opening to spring,
the shape
of a newly carved word,
is a sign

that you drink time
with your skin.

Watch carefully where you walk,
over those stones,
between faces;
there is a golden snake
growing
from the nape of your groin,
the shadow

of a woman
with scales on her gown,

or roses
killed by the same wind
that boasts
under your smile.
Moth and tiger, the pattern
chooses
to make a circle

of lines crossed with brown
fire, and yellow
snow;

wherever you go,
inside your belly
or over the moon,
I follow you, looking for wet
firecrackers,
looking
for bears and poems

frozen
behind your tongue:

Expect me soon, like a foot
waiting to stamp
the leaf
from the open flower,
a stranger, a boy
running
over new grass

and breakable
worms.

66   Real sun is what you need,
           brothers. . . .
           real sun, real girls

           who swim through the world
           with flesh growing
           like flowers
           on their bones.

           What you need is no
           paper, no
                   pictures
           hung in the private room
           behind your desk,

           no dreams becoming
           crooked
           in a box too small
           for your elbows, your arms;

           Why should you be scared to dance
           on the edge of whatever
           mountain
           you climb in the dark. . .

           when nobody else
           is there?

Approved by prophets,   **67**
annointed with bright oil from the mount
where earth lay thick as flesh
beneath the sun,
Solomon
drank God from ruby cups
long before the Oxford Movement.

Solomon
had priests who dressed for glory;
hymns broke from cymbals when they walked,
and all the world was one great tongue
tasting honey
from God's golden palm.

Long before the Oxford Movement,
little Mister Hairshirt,
mutual castration or the saint,
Solomon
bit deeply in the fabled apple,
plucked the east
to build his only temple,
and rode dark fire for his song.

68

And what dreams
do you think
I
have?
Beautiful women? Yellow horses?
Machines
bigger
than the moon?

Let me tell you
what
I dream
after all the lights
have run back into the wall,
after the last movie
on television,
when the only sound I hear
is the breath
      of my brain:

I dream of something
that pushes
me,
a thumb
pressing me down, until
there is nothing left
but water, a liquid
thickened into very special
mud, and I   flow
under my pillow
choking
            myself,
sinking
into the mattress: so

that is why
I try not to sleep, because
there will be a discovery
here,
on this sheet:
and you will scream
when I reach
for you, at the final delivery
of my
            Love.

70

Why not is
no
slogan
for serious   men;

you can hear
them
walking around
with rocks
in their pockets,

to put on the graves
of dead

spiders.

They hang around   zoos
of crooked
unicorns, objecting
to
berries, and
sleep

with iron pots
between
            their toes.

Serious   men
eat
thorns
with other people's
            mouths, and
sing
the virtue of
trimmed
glands; their shorts

are whiter
than any shirt,
and in the rain
they carry

umbrellas

painted with the name
of God.

72

1.

    Everything is distance,
space:
it waits there
in the hollow part of your eye
like a jar,
a white
jar
filled with brains,
freeways
leading to the topsecret
factory
of God: a container
to hold all the poems
that were ever
squeezed
on the street where you die,
a line in air
marking the borders
of your breath.

2

The air is filled with
blue lamb-chops,
mice,
and television sets
wired
to the inside
of our arms:
we are all tuned to pictures
reminding us
that we smell, chrome
mini-skirts caught in the machinery
of love, and
poets
drowning
in their own beards,
making kettle-drums of their mouths
and beating their
skins
behind supermarkets.

3.

How do you carve
nothing
into the shape of stars?
How do you tell your neighbors
to drive carefully
over the blacktop roads
where you left
bits
and pieces
of your private nails?
Who walks there, dreaming
of tigers,
while dogs raise their legs
in his hair?

4.

Never mind: here is a cookie
made with strawberries
and gold:
let it lie on your tongue
and melt into whatever
shape
the dancing atoms of your days
desire: let it dissolve
into magic
bones, and drip
into blessings:
open
your lips
to the wax
pouring
down your throat,
and drink that smoothness, lingering
for a while
to remember the taste. . . .

For Marinkee, with Oysters

76   Wisdom?
      your hair
      pulled over your smile,
      and a fire
      turning the rough parts of dreams
      to velvet,

      hints of some question
      dancing
      on the surface of this,
      now: each kiss the shape
      of rings
      tossed on blue candles,

      a carnival contest
      where everybody
      wins,
      and the rabbits
      move slowly
      up hills of paper grass. . . .

      (on your mouth
      there is a stretching
      of soft
      dark, like a little girl
      swallowing
      honey)

The Piper

I took her because . . .
                        because
she was there, like a stone
trying
to become a plum;

because
when she laughed, her mouth
filled
with crooked bubbles,
like elbows
waving in the sky;

because
she was trying to make poems
out of toys: blue-
eyed
dolls, and plastic
                        flowers
growing in her plush. . . .

I took her because
her voice
            (funny
as glue)
stuck to my face

and hurt me.

78

Blue trees
misted to a shape
of terror
are not to be planted by
peacocks   crotching
cabalistic tales,
nor by their wives
bearing ghetto-myths
for souvenirs: a banner of happy
testicles
nailed to doorways.

    O where are the sweet singers
    of the Bronx?

Wheeled
matzoh-balls, they celebrate
Old Traditions
and mystic candles,
rolling across the continent
delighted
with the lack of Jews;
into the pink mouths of
    THE REAL AMER I CA
they spit
bits of strudel
cooked by Momma, lovable
from an aesthetic
distance.

    Where are the wandering singers?
    Where?

In new temples
brooding on Buber and his grapes,
holding
      Grand Concourse
with keepers of degrees. . .
fiddling
with Chagall, and altaring
exotic noses.

Their wives sell translations,
husbands,
         poems
to *goyim* so guilty of existence
that every Semitic dream
becomes a Song
of Solomon, pomegranates
squeezed by dark
harpists: and
by the waters of the Pacific
they praise
     the possibilities

of Exile.

80

Swallowing the he-man
special breakfast
I
observed
waves more powerful
than saints, and

reclining

we shared
a delicious tremble
of Nature:

Christmas
pinned
under glass.

Everybody's nails
gleamed a *chupeh*, a canopy
of black stars

where God
married the sea;

trees bent
to the left hand of dark
unburdened
by any bride

or wise men
pro-
     claiming
gifts
for the birth of time:

Curious, the way
white birds
feathered the sea,
standing

on driftwood, serious
as bishops
under the wind.

82

Proliferation of torn
jaws: burning fleas
plucked from the follicles
of dead men, camels, beasts
drowned
in all the seas of the blood. . . .

It never stops, that movement
of arms, legs: a jelly
of screaming particles
trying to bite the horizon,
a stew
of bones melted into sand.

Look: they hang like pukeworms
from the open caves of their teeth,
and bayonets lift their eyes
higher than the stars:
they dance
on boiled glands.

Who cooked the world?
Who eats it?
Who labours there, in the sweated
kitchen
of the soul, fueled
with his own grease?

Lobsters

Claws are green
as sea-dream
waves that tremble
on the windows of my mouth.

Neither silence
nor need of white fingers
shaped to leaves

(as though a single eye
growing
on a stalk
could see the stars)

defines my name, or
yours.

Who would be
a stone among feathers,
a dwarf
among tall women?

Here is my brother:
he moves silent
in a tank of metal,
his dreams
heavy with horn,

his chains
dripping with the tide.

84

Lovers
look for nuggets
under their wings, small
feathers
stroked by the wind,
and bones
        empty
as space.

You can see them
float
over gravel roads,
trees, or houses where
        last year's
guitar-players
pluck television wires,
staring
at the moon.

Lovers
make fun of fences
and stones;
they wander between bright
leaves
shaking tulips
on washing-machines, and

they praise fire-
flies
that nest
        forever
in their mouths.

Any night, behind
the patio and Japanese lanterns,
a view of
goats
chewing on mountains
or mortgaged wives,

Lovers
talk to each other
with curious
fingers,

and hold
        green owls
in their arms.

86

A knock-kneed
nymph
in a spastic tree
hangs
on her willing
waiting
mouth;
weeds and crab-
grass yellow
every eye
for mockery of
lilies
on her breath.

So
she sits,
walks, rushes
into flesh,
dreams of blood, hopes to
slash
myopic stars,
everything hairy, red:
in her belly
a wasp,
a panicked sprawl
of lovers
broken at the claws.

The Apartment

Let no man discount those tears.
A moist appetite rests on your cheeks
like hunger on a dying mouth;
the white perfection of your nails
(ready for palm-blossoms, lovers, books)
turns tigers into sea-worms,
silence into wax,
and I – Odysseus with a broken face –
study strophes posted in the lavatory
for soul-growth, guaranteed.

"Between your sheets," I say
    (waving a magic condom)
"truth is the only perversity
    of which you are incapable"–
    and you weep polished needles at such
    ingratitude.

88

A red flower in a wine glass;
a jade-tree;
three roses in a green
vase;
a fireplace holding
the profile
of heat
on cracked brick, ashes
and bits of
unburned tobacco
waiting for wind;
and through the window

gardens, invisible
dogs, the moon
gaping
on Grouse Mountain, where
smorgasbord
is served for Californians
who come north dreaming
of Eskimos and
whales. . .

also books
            of course, and
a wife; miscellaneous
glands, their
contraction
under my pants; a Persian carpet
woven by women from
the hair
of sheep, all of them
dead;
a gold ring on my right
hand, a silver ring
on my left. . . .

There is a limit here,
a definition:
there is a strange tailor
measuring
my tongue
while it is still
inside my head:
there is a cackle in this
room, like
the Delancey Street shoemaker
who once
smelled the shoes
I asked him to
fix.

90   A witch of black earth,
        the old
                poet
        singing . . . but the sleeves
        of his skin
        itch into breath
        of yellow cats
        feeding in alleys
                there
        behind his mouth:
        a door
        opening two ways.

        Stroking his own fur
        he waits
        for fleas and ferris-wheels,
        careless birds,
        a ring of chassidim
        squeezing the last
                    grape
        from the holy night.

        Are there termites
        in the wine?
        How digestible is glass?
        The old
                poet
        feeds on wax cartons
        while the moon
        bangs
        on his teeth.

The Rival

Who was the old fisherman
drowned
in the rain?
his yellow boots
                floating
among the trout?

In silence
now
his beard
scrapes my window,
cursing the sun,
and there are
          hooks
in his eyelids.

I show him all the paper
I carry
under my shirt,
licenses
              and
                  poems, but
he calls me a false
child,

turning his green tongue
against the glass,
whispering
that I should not have
              fought him
in the river that
morning,

when our lines
tangled,
and our lures

rusted
in the wind.

Part 3

no matter how fast I run
the ice-cream man
is always
on the next block

94   "Who are those poets in homburg hats?"   ???

Me, that's who:
all of them, and sometimes
earmuffs
made of green feathers, starched
underwear, silk
condoms. . . .
what I wear on the secret fingers
of my brain (oranges, magic
turds, flowers
plucked from my own crotch)

is none of your business, you
with the pipe
hanging
from the revolution
of your last anthology. . . .

What you want, what
you really
want is to be John Wayne
with a full professor-
ship, and maybe
some paper
to wipe your soul,
by-lines
printed on the moon. . . .

Listen: that stuff coming out of your
mouth is words, WORDS;
you can eat
mortgages or real life,
supermarkets, pimples,
yellow mountains: it
still
comes out words, syllables stretched
between your holy cheeks,
a torn skullcap
under your tongue. . . .

Homburgs? Sure, and why
not? or a burnoose
bordered with dahlias,
red boots
for dancing in the carnival
of a co-ed's rump. . . .
listen: tomorrow I squat
on my grandfather's grave, and
give birth to angels;

Who is that   over there
cracking musical lice
in the corners
of his public hair?
Why is the Rabbi crying
TRUMBANIK!
                    GONIFF!
what are you doing
with that pushcart of dried poems?

96

You and I
march into each other's mouths
with leather boots:
we swallow sounds
darker
than the hollow places
under a dead man's
tongue.

This is the way we run
up the mountains of our skin,
our toes
tied together with ropes,
   our ankles
broken. . . .

Every time we reach for
each other
our fingers turn
into stones, a horizon
of empty bottles,
bills,
   something
waiting to be owned.

Between our lips
there are wars
thicker than jungles:
gasoline
burning whole villages, populations
defoliated
with the sprayed fat
of our own

necessities: what we do
here
        now, the violation
of treaties, a child
screaming

as we tighten steel ribbons
around his brain.

Liz

98
Look at the cat
sleeping on the serape
before a green pillow
with mice
in its ears,
and what do you say
                    now
        of Alabama?

My Alabama
is here, under my
own skin,
where everyday and sometimes
night
Big Daddy whips me
into ice-cream
tears,
because I am going to melt
too,

and inside your black
stockings (filling what wish?)
your pottery and folk
songs
somebody's grandmother
weeps
        crooked
in Brooklyn, dreaming
of cossacks

        and Christmas trees.

Here it is, like
bells or bubbles in the deepest
reaches
of our selves: a drunken
owl
waltzing on the knobs
of its claws.

We wave goodby
to ships pumping away
on the other side of leaves,
a coastline
of kisses and oyster-shells
falling down from
motels
with a feel
of wet grass, and something
else:

laughter, like hazelnuts
cracked
with our hips ... which is
   why
I carve your name
on the salt wood of this
unbirthday song,
   forever bringing

you
to the impossible   fact
of breath.

Whose hand?
death's? that finger
you feel
inside your cheeks?

What reflections do you see
at midnight, when
the moon
dangles, looped
in skinny leaves?

And what if there is nobody
home?

What if all the houses
have been turned
inside out,
flapping
Shirley Temple's underwear
from the windows?

For example:
when I walk down the street, I
know
that all my dreams
are Sunday-sections of
other people's
newspapers: yours maybe, or
that two-bit
drum
between your ribs;

and in drug-stores, where
I steal books,
    I have this urge
to leap from behind the candy-
counter, shouting
that complete strangers
have been making me
               up. . . .

It's no use, not even
throwing chicken-
soup
from the top
of the Vancouver Hotel:
the secretaries have umbrellas,
and God
has clouds, so
it's still a problem.
And I don't
trip.
Women? They never believe that
I
  need
      them   really   because
I notice things like hair
growing
around their eyes.

Let's face it, Bukowski:

only an oyster
can turn dirty
water
into pearls.

Jackie's One-Shot

102   Because
         I am no leaf of love
         to be cut and mounted
         in the coffin of your
         smile,

         Because
         I am more than oddness,
         titillation of a vein
         or specimen
         of sudden ripening,

         I give back your apple.
         Let it rot
         behind your teeth
         if you have numbered
         any part of me.

         Single-entry, was it?
         then the page
         is blank,
         and you have divided
                 nothing
         between the covers
         of your skin
         but a reed of dust:

         a puff of last week's
         wind.

All sorts of
oranges, seeds
of pomegranates shining
like fresh
      moon-juice, heavy
with dancing crabs
looking for tides
in the corners
of your arms, yellow
hair
floating over tree-tops
like seaweed, or
birds. . . .

It's what I like about
the coast, green
things
from Alaska crawling under
the rocks, Russian
sailors
with tassels   and stars
hanging from their
ears,
rolling down Hastings Street
with all their
glands
in their eyes,

and in Horseshoe Bay, the
smell
of oil and salmon,
Japanese dog-
fish lighting paper lanterns
under the pier, trees
poking
blue fingers
through the snow: when
the clouds
fall down from the mountains
there are stripes
of blue space in the fog,

ferry-boats and Englishmen,
and in the park
lawn-bowlers argue
gently
with penguins, who
thump among polar bears and
swans, a serenade
of transplanted bag-pipes
declaring
   war
on rhododendrons. . . .

There's no figuring this
town, anything
can float in with
the logs: used books and
ecstasy majors, Indians,
kosher salami and Danish
pastries: hookers
who wait
for French rolls
in the Italian cafe, where Luigi
imports wives   and cheeses
for Sicilian brick-
layers
with money or dreams
in their pockets.

How did it get here, this
city,
perched like a neon
thumb
on the edge of nothing?
Listen: whatever nightmare
you carry with you
tonight,
whatever tongue you use
to reach your private
taste,
remember that men have built
a magic moustache
under the nose of the Big Snow,
a trick
bigger than all the icicles
on the other side
of despair.

Are you afraid of

women?
                    animals?
the shape
of your own face
at night,
when nobody can see?

Do you feel

something
like a strange hand
on your nose

when you try to
breathe
            quietly
to keep that special dream
moving?

What ghosts
do you keep locked
in the bathroom,   wrapped
in a glass
box?

Remember
last night?   When your eyes
became a camera
pointed inside
out,
and you turned to your pillow

screaming dirty words? In the back
of your head?

Did anybody
                hear   you?

Are you sure?

108

Like cream on your eyelids
are poems and kisses,
money
and women: they drip
behind your closed
skin, and leak
into the sinus cavity
of every dream,
a discharge
of yellow IF, a moth
with tangled feet
screwing
cigarette-butts in the dark. . . .

and yet that fire
is de-
licious, a smoke
sweeter than plums up your
secret
chimney, where doves
play marbles under
their wings, and everything is
good: harvests of
fat and fried
lovers
gurgling at the taste
of your existence. . . .

What you want
                    of course
is a cosmic armchair
stuffed
with your feathers, each hair
a miracle-flower, like
dahlias
blooming from the zipper
of God, who stands
        amazed
and spreads his angels,
with your
NAME
a universal   fart
against the stars.

110

Why is a poem
an act, like my hands touching
your lips?

Not a wooden fence
or pear tree,
reasons for riots
or a zoo;

Not sheets of bills, or
accountants
complaining that God
has crooked books. . . .

The poem
moves around inside you
like a finger,
it finds all the places
where you were taught
never
to be found,

it opens your skull to
convolutions
of peculiar tastes, the shadow
of other people growing
in the world
        like grass.

To have poemed
is a kind of loving
when there is nothing to love
but the fog
that you breathe,
the echo
when you look at a window
and whisper
against the glass.

112

Surprised
        dragons,
frogs
sitting in trees, waiting
for water, and
fish
crawling up the legs
of birds,
their fins
splayed into hands, like a man
asking for beer:
or a lizard
unsure of where to evolve
next. . . .

Mountains
leaning on each other, red
as the moon, and
round villages
where all the houses
have purple roofs,
where fruit
hangs
from the doorways of women
mourning their lovers:
boys
with golden hammers
between their
legs. . . .

Don't ask questions:
look for this
landscape
under your pillow,
color the edge
of your skull green, until
you move
in a rainbow of crayons
and white
          paper.

114

Let a man scrape earth
and he becomes
something sharp, an edge

of iron
cutting through
last year's wood,

an instrument
to call down curses
on bugs
who dance in dead
trees,

away from sunlight or weeded
wives.

Turn over that stone
and you drown
in an ocean of pale

legs, zebra-
bellies, and somewhere a voice
screaming
under the grass:

Rub it away, the surface
of red
        yesterdays
when the air
sheds its skin for another
season, a
sucking of dark
under your feet, like

the feel

of a million hairs growing
inside the dirt
mouth
of God.

So much is dead here: leaves,
flowers, snails, sheep-
dung flown all the way from
Missouri

to paint the sky with rain-
bows, old roots oozing
from everybody's

measured ground.

116 Let no thunder come to them,
our flatulent fathers

   (do you remember the balloon
    we rubbed behind the Rabbi's house?)

for flesh would burst
at the touch of bright rod
that opens all the buttons of time

   (we cried for lollypops, plucking
    each other into beards)

and flesh fills their eyes, weights their blood
with vapours,
excrement of dreams

   (while Mrs. Kummel threatened us with carbuncles
    and love was warm and soapy)

that filth on the greener covers of the mind.
Who would wrestle with his God?
feel the hand upon his thighs?

   (bubbling surprise through all our pipes
    we tasted rainbows)

or drink the wind poured from beakers of the rock?
Leaner tribes with tigers in their breath
will read the Book of Darkness

   (clinging to the wobble of the wet
    discovery)

Elegy

The poet
with the red veins in her oven,
when she carried
a cooked bird down
to the child in her kitchen,
his white shoes
waxed
to the floor,

blamed it all on her father,
her husband: and
died
with a box of paper
planted carefully in her garden.

Her flames
were domestic, sad as temptation,
hot as a pet dragon,
regular
as the milkman, quick
as the yellow bird
screaming
behind the doors of her bedroom.

She built her own tombstone
without any fuss,
but when she knobbed herself
out of the world, leaving some pages
and a hundred professors
sniffing
at her underwear,

the house was filled with unsanitary
metaphor: and the basement
smelled
of her burning hair.

118

Curtains of red silk
offer unscholarly
definition when automobiles
dissolve into glowing
bugs: sunlight over *Klein's Super-Discount*
and pigeons dancing
with silver buckles on their wings
under the eaves of this Old
Dutch Estate
now promulgated into stereo-
phonic faces, the daughters
of Jerusalem and Sicily
who dream of doctors, stopping
their gaps
until trees turn Thunderbird
or plums.

Three fathoms up, I
turn and stare
through red silk, and wonder
if it is possible
to drown in sun-drops;
having stolen a key and created
this Office, a crow's nest
tilted
over books and lawns,
having born banners of Persian brass
and bits of dead samovars
arranged
between grammars,
I await your arrival, speculating
dividends of itch.

The honored Von of this
seascape world,
he of lordly vest and stolid
buttons (sewn on generations
of risen and rising no-longer-poor),
stands humpty-dumpty at the angle
of a sloping wall;
with eyes like eggs
and hams drifting into brick,
his manly testimonials
pierced
by the blue periods
of maidens whose mouths are filled
with questionable blood,
he spirit-whispers behind
dead fireplaces,
weeping wrinkles into plaster.

White stairways curve
to the Foreign Language Department
with banisters of oak
and patina of slide;
next to the water-cooler,
next to the men's room
where gargles unnatural plumbing
against ancestral beam,
next to fellowships posted
over bolts older than Columbus,
a co-ed refugee
from Midwestern dormitory rules
(returned to Brooklyn after spreading
kosher tastables against the moon)
dreams among filing-cabinets.

120   Down   down
down on the portico behind brown
doors and lions of brass,
where once the parlour
filled with apples and children
(sofas of plume and tobacco),
secretaries sit among cobwebs
and professors, plywood
and plasterboard: a chairman winking
anglo-saxon eyes at contractual
obligation: inside his head two ghosts
of yellow glass
rattle against seminars.

(And here in my crow's nest pulpit,
staring at red silk,
I listen for your footsteps
O my existential Rebecca,
the folk-songs that were your eyes:
trailing mothers and psychiatrists,
thick perfume,
guitars on your elbows
and announcements of Doom,
you will tell me of blocked orgasms
and ask me to
                Understand. . . .)

Cappelbaum's Lament

Nothing tastes anymore, and
the fault
      of course
is inside my mouth: candy
is too hard for my
gums,
and girls have holes
in their clothes, music is

a kind of twitch, like
juicy-fruit
snapped against a wall,
and no matter how fast I run
the ice-cream man
is always
on the next block.

Maybe I ought to get a motor-cycle
or Chinese girl-friend;
maybe
      I ought to stop
smoking. I would burn
my draft-card, but
I lost it four years ago
and nobody
        got mad.

122   Softly: like a man
       talking to him-
       self
       before a mirror,
       watching
       the shape of his jaw
       on glass. . . .

       Softly: like the moon
       set down
       on wet grass,
       holding the scent
       of lilacs and
       dogs.. . . .

       Softly: a stretch
       of rubber
       holding talcum-powder
       and skin, ready
       to welcome midnight
       with any guest. . . .

       Softly: the softness
       of a silver
       poison-box on your throat,
       set with filigree
       and a blue
       stone.

Let there be no gods among us,
no hundred-mouthed lovers
feeding on their own substance.
Let there be nothing of
fire, nothing of fruit
or great trees, mountains
where the goat
bends his curled horn
against the sun.

Let wild horses become cattle.
Let the arms of boys
become limbs of toads
drowned
in greasy pools.
Let the forest grow moss
on the teeth of our cities,
and darkness cover our books
with leaves.

Where are the white islands
riding on the sea?
The foam-struck, the dancer
of dolphins, the bringer of rain
and women
stretched over pillows
of blue space?

All things are blurred,
dropped like a shape of heavy air

    from thighs
    we once knew how to kiss.

124
Padded with fire, he
moves
among the
tulips
of the world
smelling his own
combustion, leaves
dancing
on the edge of his beard:
he fills a room
with steam.

Where he walks, even
stones
melt into kisses
or poems;
dreams of women boil
down into a pink
soup
under his eyes, and truth
is what he makes up
out of dirt.

Look at that finger:
it curls
around the stem
of a smile:
a worm
waiting for flowers to open
where dampness
spreads like smoke
over the grass.

Cappelbaum's Excursion

I walk
through pots of green ice-cream:
my neighbor's lawn.

Every morning
I take out my eye, and load it
with Japanese film; then
I go down to the beach and shoot
people who dance around
each other's Mexican
blankets. . . I listen to them complaining
about scabs on their hamburgers.

I walk
through pots of green ice-cream,
and breathe into my own veins.

Meanwhile, the camera goes BLACK
and white, BLACK and
white, like electric peanut shells
behind my eyebrows: a love-in
for citizens and other
epileptics. . . .

When I get to my neighbor's house
I will blow up like a carnival-balloon
filled
with cement.

126   Firmness: the meaning
of surfaces, where space
stops
at the skin of a pear,
or softest hair where it lies
just touching your face.

It is a question
of where
        we end,
the line   if there is a line
separating us   you   from trees,
from mountains, old women,
clouds, oyster-shells
and trains.

Sometimes
I look at you with the tips
of my hands
trying to find it: sometimes
once
        or twice
when you gleam
in a dream of silk at me
and the whole
world,

I think I can see it, or
when your eyes
shut
to look at the wind,
or when you sleep
with your fingers open

to grip the edge of the sky.

You:
what did you eat last night?
what books
have you swallowed, which
dreams, whose women?

What shirt
did you tear
from your brother's eyes
to hang
on that clothes-line
stretched between your arms?

Cannibal. . .
               Pirate. . .

Whose words
pierce your throat,
and why are your pockets
filled with gold
ripped
from other people's mouths?

Under your collar a fat
Nero
scrapes his fiddle
with the legs of girls
or grandmothers,

and behind your brassiere
a white bull
plunges at the moon,
    spitting
children

with the red weapon
of his love.

Acknowledgements

128   Certain of these poems have appeared in
the following magazines and journals:

Beloit Poetry Journal,
Canadian Forum,
Carolina Quarterly,
Chelsea Review,
Chesire,
Dalhousie Review,
Edge,
el corno emplumado,
Epoch,
Fiddlehead,
First Person,
Hollow Orange,
Lillabulero,
Mad River Review,
Malahat Review,
Minnesota Review,
Northwest Review,
Open Places,
Perspective,
Poet and Critic,
Poet Lore,
Poetry Bag,
Poetry Northwest,
Prism International,
Quarry,
Quartet,
Talon,
Tampa Poetry Review,
Thrust,
Trace,
Vancouver Life,
Wascana Review,
West Coast Review.